Neptune

The Stormy Planet

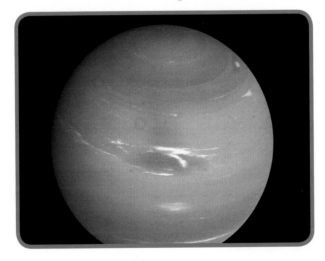

By Greg Roza

 **Gareth Stevens**
Publishing

Please visit our Web site, www.garethstevens.com. For a free color catalog of all our high-quality books, call toll free 1-800-542-2595 or fax 1-877-542-2596.

Library of Congress Cataloging-in-Publication Data

Roza, Greg.
Neptune : the stormy planet / Greg Roza.
    p. cm. — (Our solar system)
Includes bibliographical references and index.
ISBN 978-1-4339-3834-4 (pbk.)
ISBN 978-1-4339-3835-1 (6-pack)
ISBN 978-1-4339-3833-7 (lib. bdg.)
1. Neptune (Planet)—Juvenile literature. 2. Solar system—Juvenile literature. I. Title.
QB691.R69 2011
523.48—dc22

                              2010006855
First Edition

Published in 2011 by
Gareth Stevens Publishing
111 East 14th Street, Suite 349
New York, NY 10003

Copyright © 2011 Gareth Stevens Publishing

Designer: Daniel Hosek
Editor: Greg Roza

Photo credits: Cover, pp. 1, 11, back cover © Photodisc; p. 5 Shutterstock.com; pp. 7, 19 NASA; pp. 9, 15, 17 NASA/Ames Research Center; p. 13 Lunar and Planetary Institute; p. 21 © iStockphoto.com.

Printed in the United States of America

CPSIA compliance information: Batch #CS10GS: For further information contact Gareth Stevens, New York, New York at 1-800-542-2595.

Contents

Boldface words appear in the glossary.

Way Out There!

Neptune is the fourth-largest planet in our **solar system**. It is the farthest planet from the sun. We need a **telescope** to see it.

Our Solar System

sun

Venus

Mars

Saturn

Neptune

Mercury

Earth

Jupiter

Uranus

Neptune takes a long time to **orbit** the sun. It takes about 165 years to orbit just once! On July 12, 2011, Neptune completed its first full orbit since it was discovered in 1846!

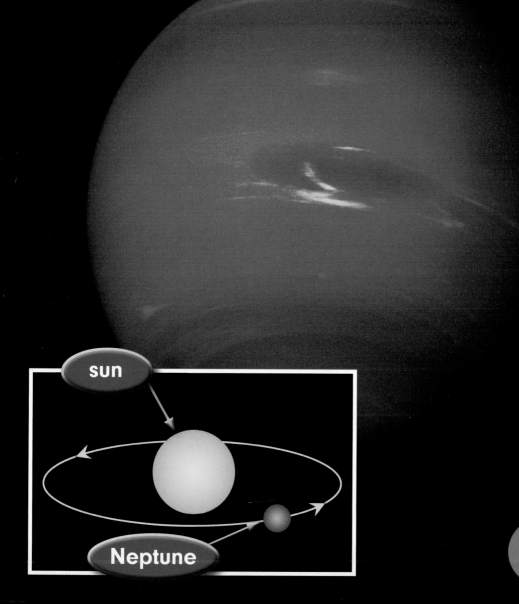

sun

Neptune

7

A Gas Giant

Neptune is called a gas giant. It does not have solid ground like Earth does. It is surrounded by thin clouds. Below the clouds is a thick **layer** of gases.

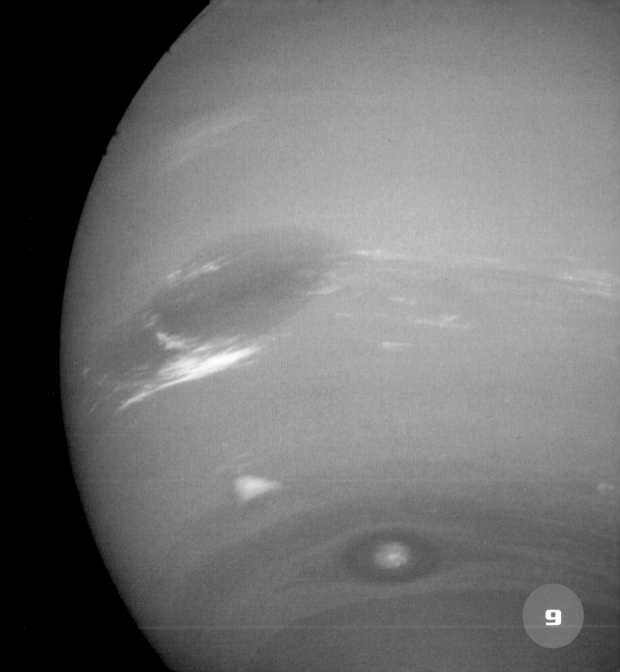

Different parts of Neptune's thin, cloudy layer spin at different speeds. The middle part makes one full spin about every 18 hours. The top and bottom parts can make one full spin in just 12 hours.

1 SPIN EVERY 12 HOURS

1 SPIN EVERY 18 HOURS

1 SPIN EVERY 12 HOURS

11

The Layers of Neptune

Neptune's outer layer is made mostly of gases. The blue color comes from the gas **methane**. The next layer is ice. Neptune's center is made of ice and rock.

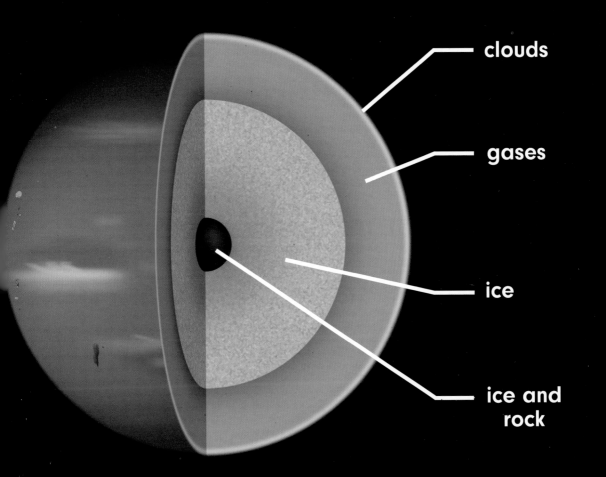

clouds

gases

ice

ice and
rock

13

The Stormy Planet

Neptune is a very stormy planet. Sometimes Neptune has dark spots on it. These dark spots are huge storms. They have very strong winds.

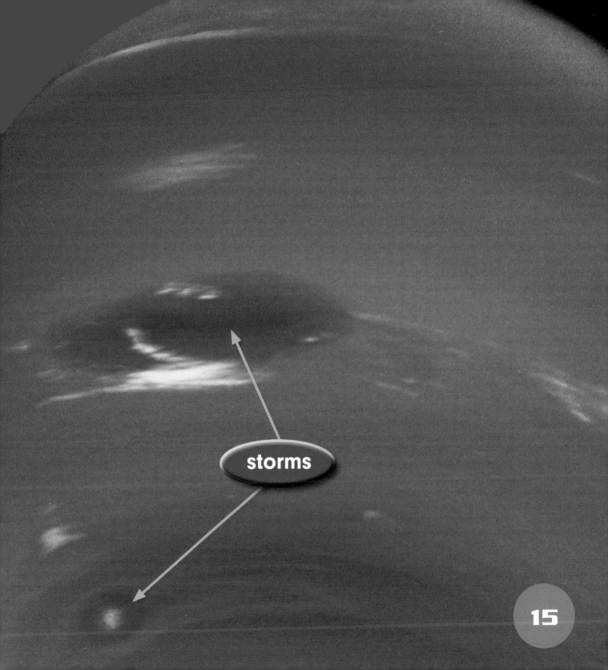

storms

15

Neptune has the fastest winds in our solar system. The planet's winds are about nine times faster than winds on Earth!

Moons and Rings

Scientists sent a **probe** to study Neptune. The probe found six of Neptune's 13 moons. The largest moon is named Triton.

Triton

Neptune

19

The probe showed scientists that Neptune has rings like Saturn. Neptune's rings are not as thick as Saturn's rings. This makes them harder to see.

rings

21

Glossary

layer: one thickness of something lying over or under another thickness

methane: a common gas in the solar system. On Earth, it is found in natural gas.

orbit: to travel in a circle or oval around something, or the path used to make that trip

probe: an unmanned spaceship

solar system: the sun and all the space objects that orbit it, including the planets and their moons

telescope: a tool used to make faraway objects look bigger and closer

For More Information

Books

Chrismer, Melanie. *Neptune*. New York, NY: Children's Press, 2005.

Loewen, Nancy. *Farthest from the Sun: The Planet Neptune.* Minneapolis, MN: Picture Window Books, 2008.

Wimmer, Teresa. *Neptune*. Mankato, MN: Creative Education, 2008.

Web Sites

Neptune
www.kidsastronomy.com/neptune.htm
Read facts about Neptune and see helpful diagrams.

Solar System Exploration: Neptune
solarsystem.nasa.gov/planets/profile.cfm?Object=Neptune
Explore this NASA Web page about Neptune, which includes facts about missions to study the planet.

Index

About the Author

Greg Roza has written and edited educational materials for young readers for the past ten years. He has a master's degree in English from the State University of New York at Fredonia. Roza has long had an interest in scientific topics and spends much of his spare time reading about the cosmos.